Full speed through the morning dark

Full speed through the morning dark

Matthew Tierney

Wolsak and Wynn . Toronto

Typeset in Calisto MT, printed in Canada by The Coach House Printing Company, Toronto
Cover design: Silas White
Author photograph: Simon Dragland

Thanks to the editors of the following journals and periodicals, in which the poems in this book previously appeared: *The Antigonish Review, Event, The Fiddlehead, greenboathouse.com, The Malahat Review, The New Quarterly,* and *Southword.* "Trans-Mongolian Express" was published as a chapbook by Mercutio Press in October 2003.

www.matthewtierney.ca

The publisher gratefully acknowledges the support of the Canada Council for the Arts and the Ontario Arts Council.

The Canada Council | Le Conseil des Arts
for the Arts | du Canada

ONTARIO ARTS COUNCIL
CONSEIL DES ARTS DE L'ONTARIO

Wolsak and Wynn Publishers Ltd
196 Spadina Avenue, Suite 303
Toronto, ON
Canada M5T 2C2

National Library of Canada Cataloguing in Publication Data

Tierney, Matthew Frederick, 1970-
        Full speed through the morning dark / Matthew Tierney.

Poems.
ISBN 0-919897-97-5

I. Title.

PS8589.I42F84 2004   C811'.6   C2004-903632

For Charmaine

Contents

HONEYMOON IN FIVE EASY STEPS

THE FACE I REFLECT / *YR WYNEB YR ADLEWYRCHAF*

THE WORD FOR *AI*

rakugaki ni / koishiki kimi ga / na mo arite

– Basho

Among the graffiti
The name of
Beloved you.

– translation, Alex Kerr

Why is everyone
looking at me?
I'm human enough.

ABRACADABRA

The window opposite
slides past the precise skyline
darkness a cloaked figure on horseback
racing alongside the train.
Bright interior light disorients me,
someone keeps tapping my shoulder.
When I turn, only rows of faces,
marionette eyes
            an absence of dust.
Maybe the Japanese understand better
the properties of illusion
how to recognise a reflection
for what it is.
I too am learning how something
can be made to disappear
with nothing more than a curtain, a word.

If she could see me now
once more
to witness this final trick.

The hands are the first to go.

Sunlit bicycles
row after row after row,
waves of chrome.

HANAMI

Each conversation another room to enter.
Eye contact passed
from one friend to the next
like a drink of water.
We listen, nod, sip.
Here, beneath a sky devoted to Spring
the four of us as perfect substitutes.
This turbulence of white
in the trees, cherry blossoms
along both banks of the Inokashira river,
                a million smiles.
        On a branch above our small talk
a crow, wick-black, begins to screech
as if proclaiming a great death
in fields beyond.
It is a relief when he flies on, heaven-
bound, allowing our pleasantries
to let out the moment.
No one notices the blossoms change.

I'm doing fine.
It's the weather
that's fucked.

THE RAINY SEASON

Some nights on the lip of sleep
I suspect I'm lucky
tumble towards voices I know by heart
the play of footsteps in the kitchen
a manner of breathing
as familiar as love.
I wake up feeling older.
There's more going on in my head
than I care to know.

Last week I smashed my umbrella
on a lamppost outside the station.
The queue for the bus watched
expressionless, playing possum.
I remember most the ringing in my skull
how I walked home carefully
so nothing would shatter.
                    Mornings now
I hum along quietly
another summer song
I've forgotten the words to.

Whisper
all her secrets
asleep.

ROMANCE NOIR

I don't know whom you've loved
but isn't it possible
they were all in preparation for us?
Tell me of withered petals
like cocoons on the carpet, wine
licked from your breasts
   the taste of California
   on his tongue.
Relive the sympathy of plush.

I imagine you sleeping.
Flicker of a streetlight outside the window:
limbs tangled in the duvet,
smeared lipstick on the sheets, hair
fanned over the pillow
   managing to look natural.
        Tell me
of the shadow stealing across your face
the space you peered through
when you opened your eyes, calling softly
to see who was there.

Trust me. If we ever meet
you'll know me by my silence.

Moon curved so fine,
an ivory handle
on a dark blue chest.

LARGHETTO

She scuffles past in pink slippers.
Her terrier, aimed with a taut leather leash,
growls. I drop my eyes
step outside the circle cast
by the streetlight.

This demon inside is whistling
kicking pebbles along the road
the moon's darker half in his pocket
one eye on the leftovers.
Leaves of the ginkgo pause when he passes.
A silver cat freezes in his path.
                    If you're lucky
you believe the lies he tells
remember a line of poetry and
circle the block once again.
Because the nights are coming
when there'll be no more to say,
our neighbourhoods so serene
only whiskey or Chopin
can make us cry.

My glass is empty.
I move the chair
to face the window.

A DRESS THAT'S WHITE

He'll ask you to keep it on,
veil too, though it scratches.
That smile, knees opening to fit his torso.
Weak hotel light dips
into your opened suitcase:
makeup kit folded into the corner,
a new bathing suit for the beach.
Room-service cart beside the curtains
sandwich crusts left aside
like unfinished thoughts.
How can I know
you won't turn your head
and think of me?

It's starting to rain here. Tap
tap tap on the windowpane, the rhythm
of a language without tenses.
I press my hand against the glass.
Such soft palpitations.

The part where I said
I didn't love you, I take back.
The rest is true.

Every language
has a word you learn
to say quietly.

SHŌGANAI

Thinking about her now
is like glancing at my watch.
How she turned me inside out
with a look, a little mustard
in the corner of her mouth,
her ears small like a child's.
She was at her most beautiful
when unaware of me
when I went to touch her, and didn't.
Once, her hand in mine,
I traced every line in her palm
with my index finger,
pretended it meant nothing.
I can count on both hands
the times we mentioned *nattō*
yet forget her last words.
I'm sorry to have to write it down.

       One more thing:
when we were under the covers
warm with the smell of each other
I always said I slept better
with her than without.
So confident in the lie.
For this too, I am sorry.

Lighted rooms.
One after another
the windows go dark.

NIGHT WATCH

In the building across from me
the man in white underwear
is doing his sit-ups.
Behind him the television flickers
like a candle near the end of its wick.
The area of his six tatami mats
the same as mine, only his.
Futon lies unmade
closet door ajar
bottle of wine on the nightstand.

Evening music
floats through screens all over Tokyo.
I'm sure if we stretched
window to window
we could grasp hands.

MANY HANDS

He who climbs Fuji once is a wise man.
He who climbs it twice is a fool.

– Ancient Proverb

*

one week after climbing season
two hours
after buses park for the night

"*baka*" I mutter
stupid
in any language

cabbies smoke on the stairs
fluorescent light gleams off
black desk phones

10,000 ¥ all I have
wallet open

the dispatcher   pencil in hand
smoothes his comb-over
right to left

*

30 minutes
of full moon
through the windshield

tires level off
mumble over gravel
Gogome   5th station

planks bar the path
orange pylons about its foot
a scatter of exclamation marks

the cabbie cracks open
his window
"Go straight"

headlights leave the trees

*

a soundless midnight
the sun to rise before five

backpack cinched up
scrambling on all fours
boulders and logs

shadows from leaves
scurry
over the forest floor

up ahead two flashlights
cavort as though
in courtship

two figures sweep past

what they must have seen
bright artificial light
off pupils

*

soaked through both shirts
wind pressing
a second skin

in each temple
at the base of my skull
an invisible grip

"Holy fuck"
inhaling now
with my mouth

the path settles
trees on either side withdraw
bowing their heads

through the gates
into a sudden arena
of night sky

in the distance the summit
like many hands
pressed together in prayer

*

to be alone
in Japan
is to find its heart

7th station within sight
shacks dark and shuttered
a tiny perch of civilisation

I rest for a few minutes
afraid
I won't start again

*

past the elevation marker
a turtled wheelbarrow

tarpaulins cover stacked lumber
spades propped
against shed walls

sawdust creeps over
windows just large enough
to reflect a face

I huddle from the wind
fork cold spaghetti into my mouth
masticate 18 times

that flicker in the periphery
my own doing
a way to keep company

*

bodies   voices
under the wooden shelter
an hour from the peak

Adidas windbreakers and cross-trainers
reflective stripes tracking limbs
through the dark

it is difficult to know
how many

university students
generous with their English
"International Relations" they say

off to the side
a pale face
sucks oxygen from a can

I join the crew
packs shrugged over fleece
zippers up in cascading harmonics

everyone tinkers
with notions of flight

*

the guy in purple track pants
paces me
away from the pack

it seems
no other shade of purple
exists

foot on stone
I frame every step
before mounting the next

each breath
a grey wafer

the sun rumbles in my chest
joints
start to drift apart

I take off my wool hat
pat down my hair
keep an eye out

like millions
before me
these last dustless steps

curious
to see who I'll meet
at the top

*

we're easy to count now
six figures
stumbling down the trail

impossible not to run
rocks fill our shoes
keep us awake

stripped to a t-shirt
day ablaze with the great things
brought forth in our absence

we can no longer look it
straight in the eye

boots kick up volcanic dust
we tie scarves around
our mouths

away from the trail
a single homemade cross
riveted to the bare mountainside

a bouquet of flowers
wrapped in cellophane
catches our sun

THE COLOUR OF *SORA*

No one wants to pack it in least of all
the foreigners. Beside me Chika
in a flush hands tucked into her lap
admirers peering over each shoulder.
Just convinced Chika to loan me
her scooter for a spin and all laugh
as though I spiked the punch line.
The beer stain on my shirt
goes unnoticed. We parade outside
six wags leading the way into a city
swamped with Saturday night. Cars
troll along the sidewalks *pachinko* parlours
sustain a full-throated gargle blue light of
each convenience store another corner
of Babylon. By the curb her scooter
one of many extending to the faint
edges of the overhead streetlight. I saddle
the cushion purple helmet squinched
on my head Chika directing my attention
to the whereabouts of the brake.
A touch of the handle *bang!* the scooter
out of the gates my pant-cuff catches on
a nearby kickstand rips and I'm down
the straightaway everyone yelling "Keep left!"
as the scooter hones in towards takeoff.
I've no idea what the natural life span
of an idiot is or how many drunks
it takes to screw in a light bulb but
true lucidity is a smooth right turn
into traffic another at the lights.
It's knowing your top speed.
A block away Chika and the others
wave I squeeze the brake somehow
twist the accelerator. The seat squirms

out from under my ass front wheel
bunts a parked scooter shooting down
an entire row like carnival ducks.
My friends rush over check the damage
a few scratches shin trickling blood.
The scooter upright again I swing my
leg over adjust the sideview crank
the gas. Leave my mark on the pavement
drone on towards the music.

Backs turned on
the morning sun
aproned housewives
sweep snow into
dustpans. It lies
fat and dreamy
until a midday
heat fills sewers
with snowmelt.
A block from
the laundromat
I pass the line
of small evergreen
trees that fence
the vacant corner
lot. The weight
of snow on their
branches topples
them so low
they seem to be
on hands and knees
kissing the ground.

Every Tuesday in this
tearoom overlooking
the station's main exit
we go over my Japanese
like a lawnmower stuck
in really long grass.
That car is big that
car is red my eyes
are grey I like coffee
clouds books yellow.
Maki assuring me
I'm doing well.
I take a sip of caramel
tea reach out and
touch the window
curious to know what's
part of the lesson.
Maki laughs. "so-ra"
she sounds it out
and I repeat "so-ra"
the word unfolding its
wings and escaping.
"*sora wa nani iro desu ka*"
she asks straight-faced
posture prim as though
we all have to bear
little tests. The question
put to me is "What's
the colour of *sora*?"
I'd be happy with
yellow I like yellow.
Ordering the same
kind of tea every
week making no
more no less headway.
Grateful now and then

when the sun interrupts
us the sudden warmth
a condition of prisons
everywhere. Below
pedestrians stream out
into the byways and
not one person looks
up. I shake my head
hopeless and Maki
says "*ao desu*" "blue."
"The sky is blue."

Ed and I find a pool hall in Tokyo's basement
down three flights an old warehouse its acoustics worse
than a chained Doberman. We grab some beers
toast eight hours at Nagoya watching giants play
rough bout after bout leg-kick leg-kick squat stare
crunch squat bow. Ed says "Remember the skinny guy?"
and leans into the first break a refreshing snap that
litters the table with possibilities. I remember a failed
attempt to soft-shoe right the sound of skull on skull
like the rip of gristle from a chicken bone. Ed
admires his moxie slides the eight ball into the side
pocket. I nod crush my empty and head for a couple
more come back penniless down two games to none.
"How'd that happen?" but Ed just grins gives me
the break. Line up stare down strike on the offbeat
and follow through. The cue ball skips over the bank
bounces twice through the adjoining game thwacks
the baseboard rolls back under both tables. Stops
at my feet. I bend over pick up the ball heart genuflecting
inside my chest. Ed snickers and bows from the waist.

The next day is a late
shift so I bring a cheap
bottle of red set it down
some distance from 2nd base.
I walk from the plate
to the centre-field fence
pacing off a home run
in my head. Back to
the bottle for a pull
I sit cross-legged my face
tilted to this evening's
stars. In all the times
I've come here no one
has ever entered this space.
Sometimes I see a figure
dart behind the visitor's
bench or a man walking a
dog along the warning track.
Maybe they sense I'm
leaving soon would rather
wait me out. I stretch my legs
lie on my back reach for
the wine. "*kanpai*" I say take
another slug wipe dribble
off my chin. Tomorrow
there might be a ball game
here. Kids in little-league
uniforms tearing around
freshly chalked base lines
the wild throw in to
the catcher. I see myself
arms raised and eyes on
the umpire cheers held
in check. Like everyone else
awaiting the call.

Something is wrong the train hasn't
moved in 20 minutes. Commuters run
off the escalators claim the remaining
spaces and if this were a boat
we'd sink. I'm buried to my neck
in Japanese my head rising clear
the first to go in a sniper attack.
Worse yet I feel a sneeze coming
and can't get my hands free.
The chime sounds at long last
the train a train again and departing.
All flirts are out of luck Mormons
too there's no room for eye contact
even a charitable thought. Everyone
breathes shallow and a pall settles.
The train rolls into the station
a little embarrassed inches towards its
mark pauses a four-count before
activating its doors. Nobody exits
passengers keeping their shape like
canned ham. Seems the salarymen on
the platform would've been better off
boozing at the bar a few more hours.
Something always gives at midnight.
An old man in a three-piece suit throws
an elbow into the wall of people and
drives with his shoulder to roll in
backwards. Nice move but hey ref
where's the call? Everybody squeezes on
somehow the doors close and we launch
towards urban myth or at least the land
of bonus questions. The next station
is an artery and if nothing else
will demonstrate the give and take
of the heart. Those who haven't heard
about tonight's two track suicides must

suspect anyway snow and death the only
things that ever hamstring this city's
transit system. It's difficult to give proper
pause knowing the victims' families
reimburse Japan Railway for each minute
of lost time. Busier lines exact higher
compensation. The rest of us are still
paying customers the train makes
all regular stops opens its doors
on cue. The outpouring is cathartic
old and young rich and poor
knocked about like clichés. An arm's length
away someone's grandmother subsists in
a state of continuous fall kerchiefed head
no higher than my waist. A student caught
in the surge turns and claws back
onto the car as though climbing
the drowned to reach the surface.
I single him out for my one prayer
not the dead or the dead's loved ones
but this boy whose tragedy is simple.
He wants to go home.

A year ago I might have
laughed. The white van
is parked on an incline
back doors secured open
ramp extended to the pavement.
Up and down men and women
of all ages carry boxes tubing
an occasional electronic
device. Such eager faces
doubts answered by a newfound
belief in deadlines. On the side
panel in black calligraphy
is *Brain Location Service*.
It's best to keep moving.

Two lunar white

Train Order Signal – Fixed signal near the entrance to a river tube, bridge, or at stations with moving platforms. Two lunar white mean *Proceed without orders according to rules....*

TRANS-MONGOLIAN EXPRESS

Beijing to Moscow
(Second Class)

*

Unpocket the boarding pass.
This may happen on a bright November morning
nine minutes before the whistle blows.
A tide of bodies under the archway, channelled between metal barriers,
each voice a white feather blown into a façade
built to withstand a revolution.
At its base a cage, a lady taking money,
the signs above her in an ancient language.
So many ways to panic. No one gets straight answers,
just the beautiful symmetry of a blank face.
Double the odds: slap a friend on the back and split up,
one carefully ripped ticket each.
Luck is born from a willingness to go unprepared
and boneheaded into the next sequence of events:
pinched scent of roasting yams, a child wailing on the stairs,
riffling digits on the arrival board.
Daylight on the platform, unfolding like memory.
Who knows how many times it could happen again,
the sun as white, the morning so offhand.
Punch a friend's arm, board a train.
Begin.

*

The motion is more insistent when we stop,
checks and balances of solid earth.
Vaughan and I feed two chunks of sausage
into the mouthlike gape at the top of the hallway window,
watch each fall wetly on the ground.
The smallest boy picks them up, stoic,
the meat held out on a flat hand.
His dog's tongue washes the palm clean.
Three dogs, four boys,
a band of mercenaries, open coats, gloveless hands,
loitering around the rail yard,
up and down the tracks as if picking along a shoreline.
The trains like the sea.
I'm not certain what kind of trouble there is
for boys around here to get into
but I wish them luck, wave and grin.
How quickly they will forget this.
We gauge how many more meals before Ulaanbaatar,
how much sausage is left
and then parcel out the leftovers,
feeling good about ourselves the way you can
from behind glass.

*

Non-stop from Irkutsk to Moscow, the longest stretch.
4 days   96 hours   5,760 minutes
that I count out like pennies from a penny jar,
rubbing each coin between my fingers.
An image hovers, hums, fades.
I'm crouched against the window in a nest
of sheets and quilts warmed by the winter sun.
On the opposite bed Vaughan's writing another postcard.
The door to our berth is closed but unlocked,
rattling in its metal tracks.
This percussive language. Four days.
The train pulling the first to the last,
snapping them shut like a purse.

*

The first thing you notice
when the train stops at an unannounced station
is noise. Creaks and knocks
passed on like code through the thin, wooden walls.
It's suddenly difficult to regulate the volume of your voice.
Passengers emerge into the hallway, uniformly slippered,
and eye each other suspiciously
as if someone pulled the plug.
Quickest to regain their wits are the smokers,
solitary figures stamping up and down the platform,
faces penitential, to conceal thoughts of escape.

        Vaughan and I stare out the window.
        "Your turn," he says, a cookie-cutter grin,
        corners of his mouth stiff as tinfoil.

What we need is ingrained
after rooming so closely with its absence,
a list I expect to recite on my deathbed.
I drop my book, throw on my boots,
don't bother with my jacket.
One leg out the exit, the wind pulls like an undertow
and away I go, untied laces flowing behind,
and it's like playing chicken with a truck, only here
not a truck but a moment.
The station is busier than you'd think,
so many people a lifetime from where they want to be.
Bahbooshkas front card tables with cupboard wares,
a few stores shimmer white
like misplaced gazebos amid the blowing snow, watery sun.
In the distance, an uncrowded one.
My feet piston towards it, arrive first in line,
pivot to see how far I've come.
I flinch, imagine the train jerking forward,
pulled on a string by some childlike god,
that last car growing smaller, smaller.

An arm's length away,
snow rolls by sunlit windows
like tiny, weightless, albino tumbleweeds.

Ah fuck—
I crouch in towards the kiosk,
point to the closest recognisable objects, Mars bars,
hold up two fingers. Friend on the train, I want to say
as if it were important for the storekeeper to know
I would not eat them both.
My left hand wrestles out a fistful of coins:
Mongolian togrog and Chinese jiao
leftover yen, a lucky loonie.
I shiver through them, collect the rubles to one side,
shoring them up along the edge of my hand like the prettiest rocks.
Wind breezes through my thin flannel shirt,
the storekeeper patiently Russian,
fate a currency he often deals in.
Twenty rubles, there you go.
The bars in my hand, I fly westward,
aim myself at the horizon.
Car numbers mark my progress
304   303   302
mission control sounding off in my head.
I brush past the conductor on the bottom step,
wheeze into the hallway, Mars bars aloft.

Down near the window, pillowed in electric warmth,
Vaughan peers at me:
"Didja get the batteries?"

I shake my head, Vaughan smiles at the carpet
and wiggles his stockinged feet.
Wrappers dark in our hands, we chew,
study the bare winter stage.
Siberia.
15 minutes
before the train hitches its skirt and ambles forward.

*

Two nights, two days,
and my voice bounces inside my head.
Sitting beside the window, cardigan unzipped,
I shift my journal so the empty page catches sunlight,
wonder how much longer my pen will last,
how many more words are in it.
There will be no more pens till Moscow,
when everything makes sense again.
Outside, snow lays hands upon the earth,
blank areas of the map that keep the names of towns apart.
It's easy to be sentimental about landscape,
how it draws a note and sustains it.
A violin quivering across fields.
Of all instruments, most closely resembling the human voice.
But sentiment is hard to string together
in one good sentence when it matters most.
With a bark of energy, Vaughan throws down *Les Misérables*,
pads into the hallway to fetch hot water.
Soon a cup's warmth is babied in my lap,
thoughts of how I got here, who I met along the way.
The sky is like a slate and on it
I draw and redraw the horizon till it suits me.
Vaughan gazes past the French Revolution:
"Crazy 8s?" he asks, dusk in his eye.
I place my tea beside the honey jar,
steam flickering on the cold windowpane,
touch the pen's cap to my lips, then write,
"Two days, two nights, voice bouncing inside my head."
I close my journal. Off somewhere in the interior.

*

There's nothing to be done.
Passing a station full speed through the morning dark,
you sense something terrible must have happened
if only because you're rushing away from it.
Drop your head back on your pillow,
close your eyes and nurse the motion.
Falling asleep again is always harder than you think.
Perhaps you recognised a figure on the platform,
face tinged the blue-white of snow,
studying each black window as it shuttled by.
With dawn comes a steady sun,
a sadness you can't place,
another name off the list
you swore you'd remember.

*

Somehow the hours go by.
Game after game of Crazy 8s on the Arborite table
that sticks out like a lip beneath our window ledge.
Just when one of us becomes convinced of his luck,
the other slams the cards back into their case.
Meals are all elbows, trading off the one Swiss army knife.
On our sausage sandwiches we drip honey from an old pickle jar
picked up for 15 rubles at the border.
It's our third day without a shower.
Batteries in both walkmans died again in the night,
that last note dropping over the edge of consciousness,
splashing quietly in our sleep.
Vaughan rips out pages of *Les Misérables* as he reads,
reciting spirited passages before throwing them away.
It seems we are constantly waking up,
going for a ciggie in the bridge between cars, that pintsize purgatory,
smoke and breath spiralling together
while we show off by writing our *katakana* names,
fingertips melting the moss-soft frost on the windows.
It's the constant tremble beneath our feet,
the sounds of Russian through the walls,
the strident midnight knock on our cabin door
and we cling to each other without ever showing it.
Watching darkness come again and again to try and stop the world.

*

Last day. Our groins are chafing.
We lose track easily now, two bellyachers
propped up by pillows, hoarding comfort.
Conversation boiled down to syllables and swallowed like pills.
The bunks opposite ours have been sporadically filled,
rueful, troll-like men that arrive in darkness,
gone before we awake, leaving the sheets in twists.
We've kept the berth locked all day,
drawn battle lines with our eyes.
Waiting for the *knock knock* at the door,
customs officials and conductors, black-market scowls,
the punch lines you instinctively want to duck:
"Open!"   "Stand!"   "Please!"
We try a friendly game of cards,
heads down, hearts slapped on the table
until the shadows under the door
hammer to be let in.

        Vaughan glances at me, a last wisp of privacy
        before reaching out and sliding back the bolt.

Two men bustle inside, hats bigger than their heads,
gear pushed ahead of them in well-travelled bags.
Garrulous as drunks on a shortcut.
Vaughan hops over the narrow aisle to side with me,
flying roo-like onto the top bunk
and they keep glaring at us
as if to figure out whom to blame for what.
Misha is the one to plunk beer on the table
though at that moment we didn't know his name
nor imagine it could be important to know.
Tomas unwraps the package of fish,
black and oily, each the size of a thumb,

their smell immediate, intoxicating.
He lays them on the backside of a paper bag,
invites us to eat and drink with king-sized gestures
as though playing to the back of the room.
We have nothing to give them
other than our hunger, an idiom or two,
squeezing out introductions between mouthfuls.
Misha owns a few English words
and tosses them into the air like coins
that each of us leans forward to catch.
We name things. Open our second beer.
Vaughan and I know enough now
to say *spahseebo*, tongues like banana peels,
tipping our bottles towards the light, smiling in Russian.
Vaughan grabs my journal, turns to the back,
writes down words as though pinning them to the page.
Train, *poyenzd*.   Woman, *gensheena*.   Gun, *roozhyo*.
To ask for an ashtray, *pyepyel-neetsah pozhahlooshtah*.

Vaughan and I look at each other, narrow our eyes:
This is good stuff, we can use this.

Tomas dramatises his job, pointing his index finger at us
and firing. "Poleetsa," he says.
Misha pushes his thumb into his chest: "Meelitia."
Our friends, the biggest kids on the block.
We knock back a last beer, head down the hallway for a ciggie,
pass the *zhaba* conductor, "dragon-lady"
we say to her back, wink at each other.
Pass too those wintered men deep in their berths,
doors open as if to welcome a challenge.
No time left to stare them down.
One by one we're through the exit,

always a balancing act, the cars jostling for position,
metal sucker-punching metal.
Down the line, Moscow keens faintly
as Vaughan lights everybody's cigarette,
four floating periods for the words left unsaid.

The write-up says this section of the Wall is the most dangerous. We decide
to climb it. Like most people, we have no concept of danger, only fear.
And who's afraid of a pamphlet? Halfway

up the path is a metal sign.
Once
luminous white, now mottled with rust, this struggle of order and chaos
rages from season to season. Five red Chinese characters hold forth their
many limbs. Beneath them in English:

PleasePay attion tothe safty.
Difficult to guess how long the sign has been here, doling out its nugget
of wisdom under a great shadow. Such sufferance. I'm sure our safety
will get no attention

till it's compromised. We catch our breath, gaze out
over the furrows and folds of bare hills, earth gathered like a blanket along
the horizon. Despite the wind, it's tempting

to wait. Beauty always tenders
its final shimmer. But with walls, where you stand means picking sides.
Signs can also be read

on the way down.

Northern China

A portrait of Mao looms over the entrance to the Square, the mole
on his chin a foot in diameter. Somebody
                        had to paint that. On
the bridge, young men in military costume chatter in groups, blow
smoke into the evening air. Vaughan and I
                        duck their glances
as we cross. Last thing we want is a history lesson from a teenager.
Under the passageway, echoes swoop from recesses high in the ceiling's
corners. We're through onto bleached cobblestones
                        a spotlight, a path
that leads nowhere special. Soft curl around the guardhouse, shadows
thrown from the windows like pails of
                        water, taking shape on the ground.
Our steps soundless, we pass the men inside, swallow uneasily. I make
fists and withdraw them into my sleeves, the fingers of my gloves thin,
lifeless. Within a few minutes we find
                        the quad, closed for construction.
Along its bottom, beside the single, fixed light, a hooded silhouette floods
the mucked earth with a hose. It feels as though at any moment the tide
could come in. We stand
                        ten minutes. Vaughan opens and shuts a Mao-
faced lighter, bought last night because it plays a tune.

Beijing

In midstream I hear barking, my back to the sidewalk, steam rising
from tiny flues in the snowbank. I manage to
                           cut it off, something I never
thought possible. The dog is behind me, having a go at Vaughan. Zip up,
button, buckle, check the luggage and
                      take off. Foxtrot the first few
metres, dog nipping at our jeans, then assume a mosey. Was just a pup
but man, I nearly pissed my pants. The air is chill
                       the dusk blue, falling
behind apartment buildings in faint sibilants. A bus grinds up and over
the hill, leaving exhaust in the space
                  between road and sky. A backdrop
of huddled brick. Smokestacks. Night approaches like the Black Forest,
shops close their blinds one by one. We find a drugstore still open, pull
the handle and enter. The bell-chime
                  bewitches winter on the doorstep.
We unbutton our jackets, unwrap scarves, shake out snow. Above
the counter, a clock blinks towards the top of the hour. The clerk is old and
haggard, printing the day's transactions. A couple with gloves laced together
cock their heads
               in perfect accord. An unaccompanied woman stands tall,
quiet, homely. Four people. The trick is to figure out which one is real.

Irkutsk

Customs, a gutted church. The scuffles of past congregations echo
in the feet of travellers looking beyond
                             the border. One Mongolian man
in a regal *papakha* is denied passage, his boxes of jean-jackets confiscated.
A lesson to us all. Bury your contraband
                           deep in your heart. I surrender
my valuables, stand before the glass partition, arms limp at my sides.
The soldiers lean over my papers as though deciding just punishment.
Waved on, out the exit, luggage
                      in the care of Mother Russia, we enter
a village lulled by the sun, mill about the open-air market, a dozen tables
with winter clothes and comic books, small appliances, bread, honey.
We sift through necessities. Past the gates
                      a cloudless afternoon, no name
for this place. Along the outskirts of town, rays skim between trees, cracks
in so many curtains. We start through the grove, emerge at an old rail yard,
roam the empty cars. Discover a locomotive from the 40s, its body rusted
and seized up like an old rifle. We brush snow
                    off its wheels, take a step
back. Vaughan. Me. Standing on the ties.

The last of our rubles. We stare at our beer, finding truth in effervescence,
its ability to filter the room. Somehow
                              we've run out of options. Walked
for an hour, streets wide and vacant and the wind not much for song.
It's Saturday night, the bar small, windows fogging up. Patrons
either coming from or going to
                              a better time, almost certainly by car.
We've only got Plan B, tough to pull off with a near-empty glass. We trade
hypotheticals, swirl our dregs. Then
                              as the joke goes, a monkey
saunters in wearing a diaper. The owner lifts it onto the empty stool
beside me. Sets out an array of sliced oranges. It's difficult not to be
impressed, especially when you're this hard-up
                              for ideas. When you've never
touched a monkey before. We're told it's a she, the grip strong, cool,
inhuman. She turns to the oranges, pushes some to the floor, squirts juice
over her face. Her owner patiently offers up a napkin. The monkey takes it,
clumsily dabs at her lips, and we're all
                              charmed, I'm sure, holding applause
in our hearts. How far
                              we've come. Opposable thumbs curled around warm
beer, foreign currencies. Every bipedal step an adventure of selection.

Moscow

The hours before leave-taking are slow and unwieldy. Sooner or later
we should return the things we borrowed. Breathing space. Gravity.
Hotel towels. We wander
                        incandescent streets, happen upon an imperial
building behind an iron fence, frozen pond within its square. One corner
is shovelled. A never-ending game of shinny hits overtime. We test
the surface while kids skate
                            around us, scratching paths to glory. Vaughan's
never seen natural ice and is unfamiliar with its sense of humour, its spit
and polish. We return to the bank, fit boots into their original imprints,
tramp to the pond's centre. It's snowing
                                        much heavier now. On the far side
sits a snack bar, closed for the night, wooden deck arcing over the pond.
Seen this in a Bond film, almost positive. But Vaughan's no help. He's
taking his turn, a running start towards a thin stretch of ice surrounded
by three boys. Push off
                        and soar. At the end he jumps too late, stumbling
to his knees. The boys laugh, Vaughan winds up for another try. Still
plenty of time. Flakes catch in his eyelashes, weigh down his shoulders.

Moscow

We'd planned only one night but slept past checkout three days in a row.
Each noon awake to the fact
                    we pay for our mistakes. It's off-season,
the hostel half vacant. One guy has been here eight weeks or forever,
depending on whom you talk to. Vaughan and I hook up with two women
from Sydney, meander each day on the outskirts of town, throw snowballs
under a blue-eyed sky. Night
                    comes and we're at the snake bar. The usual
table of English speakers, some shot glasses, a bottle of absinthe legal only
in the Czech Republic and Spain. Makes you wonder
                    what's so special
about Spain? We swallow languidly, run fingers beneath our eyes, follow
shadows on the wall. Midnight. Feeding time
                    for the constrictor in the back,
asleep under a heat lamp. Heads turn, bodies crowd the glass tank, blocking
our view. I slip into another conversation with the separatist from Montreal,
try and change the topic to hockey. Hours later
                    we shake on it, switch
venues, burn bridges. Return to brush our teeth at first light. If we vomit
in bed, the notice says we "loose our key deposit." Vaughan squeezes
toothpaste onto his finger and transforms the two Os into a grinning face.

Cesky Krumlov

Honeymoon in Five Easy Steps

Keep an eye
out for sham-
    rocks. Tip one chamber-
    maid in every four. Press
          overpriced smiles between leaves of
          a guidebook, let each moment turn-
                    stile into the next. Plan
                    two ahead. And god bless
                              such dumb luck
                              to have and hold.
                              (X)_____
                              (X)_____

FROM "I DO" TO THE NATIONAL GALLERY OF IRELAND
IN 36 HOURS PLUS 12 EXTRA-STRENGTH TYLENOL

aon

The wheelchair idea was your brainchild, and it's not
        playing so nice. My knee though
is swollen, my heart sore at being yanked
        off centre stage. You try to make it fun,
experiment with terminal velocity from check-in
        to departure lounge. But I know
what you're doing – putting the cart before the horse.
        First on the plane, first off, small
consolation. In Heathrow, my pain got bumped
        to first class. An hour to locate a chair, wheel
to our connecting flight. I think how I miss
        critical decisions: stop/go, left/right, step, shuffle,
shimmy. How the next chance I have to walk
        onto a plane, I'll run.

dó

I awake propped on a cushion of
        acetaminophen. Nine, dark out. A single bulb burns
atop the dresser, suitcase open on a chair, offering
        its finite alternatives. This room of ours,
two flights above O'Donaghue's pub, overlooking a street
        from "The Dead." In the mirror your face,
tilted, camera-ready, while the right hand
        tugs a line of colour under an eye. Too easily
are these moments dismissed. I hesitate
        to stretch, afraid any noise
will alter the course of your attention; watch instead
        lamplight fall
through the window and stay.

trí

I guess the joke's on me when you jam
        my protruding foot into the lift door, reverse
and try again. Anticipation gums up my jaw. Ah,
        sticky moments, second thoughts, that video loop
of my leg crash-landing on the dance floor:
        ryengingerloosentiemeup,
russianfolkgonnadropkick-me-down, full stop.
        To the present, band-aid quick, gliding past Yeats
painted by a Yeats, brand-spanking wife
        pushing me around the corner. Not for the first time
I say, "In sickness and in health, baby!" and still
        you laugh, my constant, my speed
of light.

SELF-GUIDED TOUR OF ST. NICHOLAS TRIGGERS
A MEDITATION ON WHAT WE LEAVE BEHIND

aon

Three dinosaur-sized scaffolds. Milky plastic sheet
        along the perimeter of the nave, a shroud
to all but the most curious. Shame to cross
        an ocean to find this; but then Ireland boasts
many steeples. Point of pride.
        We drop euro nickels into a wooden box,
take the dime-store tour, feature to feature
        as though wheeled along a clothesline.
A tombstone pans into view: Jane Eyre (?), careful
        and indulgent, left 300 pence to be "distributed
in bread to 36 poor Objects every Sunday
        for ever." Dead at 88, simply alive
before then.

dó

Window seat in a coastal town, this café
        the size of a walk-in closet (with fireplace).
Outside, inches from the rain-streaked glass, a woman's
        face: whiskered chin, tongue like a flipper, wart
that says it all. I wink, she
        calls my bluff – in seconds a lily green slicker
abuts the edge of our table, her outstretched hand
        shaped like the cheeky end
of a monkey wrench. "Norma!"
        Flat out from the kitchen, the owner corners her
by the front door. "I'm nice to you, Norma, don't
        try that passive aggressive shite."
I continue to stare long after
        she retreats into the rainscape.

trí

Galway oysters, the squabble while parking the car, laundress
     who knew how to spell our name
without asking. Maybe too this last-gasp lap
     around St. Nick, looking up to glimpse a gargoyle
looking down. The grass is spongy, it's starting
     to rain, and a coffee'd be nice before
we realize our passports still lie
     in the bottom drawer of the night table
on Inishmore, waiting for us to recover
     covered ground. You can't choose
what to remember about a place.

GALLARUS ORATORY AMID FOG AFTER GUNNING
AROUND DINGLE PENINSULA IN RECORD TIME

aon

My boots scuff the dirt floor, eyes
        adjust to the sink of 1,300 years,
corner to corner no more than ten metres, the peaked roof
        a pivot and jump away. Outside,
you troll the mounds and metamorphic rock,
        drizzle weighing down your hair and
I imagine I feel you, as one feels hope or occasionally
        time. How difficult it is to be alone anymore.
Ahead of me is a thin window that lets in light
        from the end of day; promise
of love to come. My eyes dilate slowly. A thousand years ago,
        yesterday, tomorrow, it's all one.

dó

Arrived just in the nick. Another 15 minutes will bring
        darkness, heavy rain and regret. Early Christians
must have learned this too. Punctuality, next to
        cleanliness and a sharp blade – the only tools at hand
to govern fate, to deem
        any of this meaningful. The ticket-taker gone
home, a blank-windowed kiosk to greet our return,
        our coupe (a rental) in the car park
alone. Chorus of dead languages off the Atlantic,
        the notion that believing is no more
than seeing our future selves materialise
        on the path ahead, steeped in mist.

trí

We can't even plan an afternoon's drive, never mind
        a gritstone hut, waterproof still
after 13 centuries of devilry and mayhem. People
        used to congregate here, despite the square footage.
People shorter than us (judging by the entrance), breathing shallow
        in the presence of their God. Maybe it's just this
that frightens you: one of them
        left behind, huddled in the east gable, picking at scabs,
charged with warding off would-be spirits
        in a darkness both superstitious and real.
Such capacity for sorrow. Now I understand
        why you leave to explore the grounds.

DÚN AONGHASA (ANGUS' FORT) LOOKING WESTWARD OVER
AN ATLANTIC THAT REMINDS ME OF OUR KITCHEN FLOOR

aon

I'm not prepared for the drop of it, sheer 300-foot
    inevitability. Such a clean line between
being here with you
    and not. The wind is stubborn, though no match
for stupidity. It's a wonder tourists aren't lost
    in alarming numbers, one by one. You and I
worm out towards the cliff, poke our necks over
    the edge. Below, the reason for it all.
The sea swirls in great apostrophes while a roar
    fills my hood, floats it
like a flag. To impress you, I spit, and the wind hurls
    the attempt back and up (thankfully)
over my head. The constancy of nature, I muse
    as you hiccup with laughter, out of place
but attached all the same.

dó

Who Angus was
    is unknown. There are two possibilities:
a man who belonged to a high-ranking dynasty or
    the King of Cashel. I imagine him a series
of concentric circles, cranium like an overturned pot,
    cylindrical ankles. Sucking a plug of gravel, switching it
cheek to cheek. Shakes hands at every leave-taking.
    His wife would (of course) know things about him
he's unaware of, and after another nine to five
    putting his name to a belt of rocks that'll last
beyond our lifetimes, he'd stand with her where
    I am now, a king or just a man
peering west over marbled, limitless green.

t008tt

trí

We're still airplaning, stomachs cool on the damp rock,
    wind force-feeding our lungs. To our right
a step-high altar; step two, kingdom come.
    Four dull, bronze rings were found buried
with purpose beside it, an offering to some almighty
    who demands such things. A god of
hardware. Maybe
    the ceremony went something like this:
a row of flattened celebrants, arms wide-open, heads
    tucked against sea spray. Whatnot
lovers. Every excuse to act like idiots,
    tongues in one cheek, hearts in the other.

BUNRATTY CASTLE AND IS THAT ERROL FLYNN SWINGING
FROM THE TORSO OF A MERMAID CHANDELIER?

aon

Straw mattress in the servants' quarters. Beside
        the hearth a well-placed kettle. Headroom's
a problem, view of the grounds
        pinched. Other chambers are ripe
for the picking: portraits and tapestries, rare virginals, damasks,
        leuchterweibchen – mermaids chained
to the ceiling. Still, easier to imagine being poor
        and overworked, paused at a chink in the staircase
to spy on the Earl, his gout-ridden friends,
        that constant whisper
in the Great Hall. *Enough*. Hot coals in the bed-warmer,
        wife boiling a leg of mutton, the long
medieval night. I turn from the high collars, battle plans
        creeping over the oak table.

dó

Interior walls are whitewashed, dungeon
        on up. Twice nightly, local talent look the part
in the world-famous Bunratty Medieval Banquet.
        Hearty food, flowing wine, chivalry! Not to mention
rampant gonorrhoea, negligible
        plumbing. When in history did we first get
the money-back guarantee? Like any child
        grown fat on creams and cakes, we could use
a royal caning. (Ladies first.)

trí

Details: like paint-by-numbers when the digits
        are too small. What I know is what I feel.
Bum knee. Tap of cane on stone. The top of your head, snug
        under my chin. It's late, the castle closing
at four. Ghost-tasting Guinness, I hobble along,
        cap in hand, squint-eyed
for a flash of movie magic. Looksee, the turtle shell hanging
        like a beer gut on the kitchen wall, clocks
wrist-deep in gears, a 15th century cupboard with salacious
        writing flap. Thankfully, you take no imagination
or you take all of it. Either way
        I'm thirsty and follow you everywhere.

THE FACE I REFLECT / *YR WYNEB YR ADLEWYRCHAF*

As has been said,
the point of travelling is not
to arrive, but to return home

– R. S. Thomas

The years thumb-printed
in the hollow of his throat, hands unearthed,
ungainly beneath the hard light
of this kitchen. Coffee steams before us,
darkness rough against the window,
heavy winds and freezing rain.
Sometimes he forgets I'm here,
eyes lost to films of thin yellow,
staring at something more interesting
than a man he doesn't know.
                                        His voice
stumbles over old ground like a drunk
heading home at dawn,
home to him a small Welsh town
somewhere beyond my left shoulder.
I picture a valley, morning sun spilling
over the heights of trees, rooftops,
shingle to shingle and leaf to leaf
like water, soaking red earth,
breaking upon rock. The sea barely
a thought, miles away,
scrubbing salt into the wind.
                                        He raises
his mug and tugs at his coffee, wipes
the backs of fingers across stubble, a thin sound
that turns in my ears. Again his hands,
hoary jaws that once lifted me
into the air, a knuckle to three ribs,
the small of my life, to him
just another side of winter.

                    Now slow,
dog-eared words fall open before me,
my grandfather, ten years old, visiting his own
in a grainy room somewhere in some
dim crack of Ireland. A bruise of a man,
sodden eyes and fallen arches, sitting too long
in pubs after work, right arm like an oak branch.
He could lay out any man
who asked for it. But for his grandson that night
a lesson on the fiddle, ending with that arm
bending the wood of a homemade bow,
strings close to breaking
but never daring to, windows humming.
                                        And I turn
to catch my likeness in the glass.

SKIDDAW MOUNTAIN

The blood on my knuckles
makes my skin itch. One hour
after my nose begins to bleed
                    I give up
tumble into the heather
like diving into snow.
The silence up here has eyes.
I balance my centre of gravity
on the incline, throw a pebble
            high into the air
listen to it fall all afternoon.
A raven flies by at eye level,
wings rippling the sky –
blue thinning to white, the sun
inches from my fingers
when I stretch my hand.

Keswick

R. S. Thomas

I press your words
into my palms, here –
a garden of wildflowers
penned by a wrought-iron fence.
        Outside, the machine clicks on,
the city your birthplace
not your home.
For you, the portion of sky
    that remains unseen
        behind the hills, calling
on those who live beneath it,
kitchens warm with the smell
of bread: tufts of cloud pinched
by peasant thumbs. You came
to learn their language, not speak it,
a courtesy I return to you.

Cardiff

RAIN

Such a long way to be surprised.
Each vacant storefront I pass,
a broken window slices
        another piece of my reflection.
People are seen only
from a distance, mumbling
to themselves like priests.
Grandad was born into this?
        No. Something happened
here and time kept going,
licking the nails of boarded inns
to rust, leaning on brick
until it cracked like bone.
        Every step
brings me closer, rain washing away
my tracks. It's happening still.

Newport

I see him with eight-year-old eyes:
summer, the tidy coughs
of his moped, red-speckled helmet
bobbing against a monochrome sky.
Seldom in a hurry, he moved through
scenes like a brush on canvas, sure
each picture would finish.
      At night banging toys into shape
in his workshop. Coaxing tin tobacco
into rolling papers, cigarettes
piling white magic
on the kitchen table. Those hands
never flinched, never lost
their grip
          never touched
what he couldn't see, the memory
of my face deep within their creases.

Newport

IFTON STREET

The Pakistani boys chase
cricket balls under parked cars.
"It's their neighbourhood now,"
 my second cousin's husband says.
"Was different for your grandsire."
                              But Grandad
was a boy once too. I leave
before dusk, pause under
the battered street sign; watch two kids
make their way towards me.
                    "Spare a fag, mate?"
I shrug, apologise. For a while
I'm different. They talk till
there's nothing to say, then recross
the road, restless to do something
mum and dad shouldn't know.

Newport

BECALMED

Beyond the wire fence
boats lie on wooden props,
each spaced respectfully
from another, primary colours
dying in the sunlight.
The dimensions of the shipyard
endless.
       Wandering takes me
only so far. Behind the chained gate
a blue-collared angel finishes
the day shift inside his shack.
I stare through metal links,
the afternoon framed by diamonds.
       Notes ping from a radio
as if played at the bottom of the sea.

Swansea

IN BETWEEN

Neither morning nor
afternoon but in between.
On the downward turn of the road
I discover the valley's pearl-
blue waters, pick up my stride
in response to the current.
          The hills embrace
a familiar sadness here,
crags and leafless trees
pockmarked with superstition.
Farmers lock their doors
at the approach of footsteps, wives careful
to stay behind curtains. Stray dogs
know to keep their distance.
          I wonder how many of us
shyly remember tears,
continue walking towards god.
The river folding once more,
                    claiming its own.

Conway

BURDENS

The hair curls over his lip
so tough it grates against
the teeth of the scissors, falls
in slivers onto his shirt.
I line another length along
the lower blade
       imagine the skin I open
       when tip meets tip. Pray
for accuracy in slowness.
Grandad lives without humour
now, closes his eyes to life's tasks.
Waits for the pressure of
a grandson's hand to tell him
which direction to look.
       I squint, lean close
but nothing comes clearer, no
thoughts, none of the darkness
he dreams in; only a face
I might recognise, in time.

Marmora, Ontario

Acknowledgements

"Many hands" is for Steve McOrmond.

THE FACE I REFLECT is in memory of George Tierney, 1912–2003.

Utmost gratitude to Steve McOrmond and David Seymour, for the years of editorial insights and unfailing support. To all those who had a hand in these poems, thanks and thanks again: Adrienne Barrett, Brooke Clark, Ben Kalman, Janet McOrmond, Myron McShane, Maki Mineo, Griffin Ondaatje, Craig Proctor, Sue Sinclair, Murray Sutcliffe, Andy Weaver, Richard Weiser, Silas White, Mark Young, and all members of the Icehouse Group, circa the heyday of grunge. And to Vaughan Marshall, for letting me believe I'm half of "the best Aussie–Canuck duo ever."

Love to my parents, Fred and Theresa, for giving me every chance in the world, and also to my godmother, Pauline Dietrich. Finally, to my wife, Charmaine: I couldn't have done it without you. All my heart.